Original title:
Blossoms of Brilliance

Copyright © 2025 Creative Arts Management OÜ
All rights reserved.

Author: Lorenzo Barrett
ISBN HARDBACK: 978-1-80567-014-8
ISBN PAPERBACK: 978-1-80567-094-0

# Fields of Light and Color

In the meadow where the sunshine plays,
Colors dance like they're in a craze.
A purple cow wearing a polka-dot tie,
Sips lemonade, oh my, oh my!

Butterflies giggle, they jump and flap,
Twirling around in a lovely nap.
Bees buzzing tunes, like a marching band,
Funky moves in a flowered land!

Daisies wear sunglasses, feeling so cool,
While tulips play hopscotch, it's the new rule.
Grass giggles softly beneath our feet,
Joyful chaos, oh what a treat!

In this carnival of colors so bright,
Every petal beams with sheer delight.
Nature's jesters in a vibrant spree,
Laughter blooms, wild and free!

## **Petals of Radiance**

In the garden, a daisy wears
A hat made of socks, oh what a pair!
Sneaky bees with tiny grins
Dance around in silly spins.

Tulips chatter, sharing news,
Of how they once lost their shoes!
Laughter blooms in each small bud,
As daisies puff, looking like thud.

## Whispering Colors of Dawn

The sun tiptoes with a wink,
Painting skies while herbs just stink.
A rooster's got a busy role,
Squawking tales to wake the whole.

Bluebells giggle, swaying light,
Telling jokes to worms at night.
A rainbow sneezes, colors spray,
And clouds all giggle, 'Hip hooray!'

## The Garden of Luminescence


In the moonlight, the veggies prance,
Carrots try to lead the dance.
Radishes wear sparkly shoes,
While lettuce sings the rock 'n' blues.

Cosmos twirl in stealthy flight,
Winking at the starry night.
They chuckle as the fireflies,
Buzz 'round their heads in funny ties.

### Hues of Serendipity

In a patch of wild marigold,
A dandelion tells tales bold.
It spins yarns of a petal race,
Where roses slipped and fell from grace.

The bright sunflowers wear their shades,
Sipping dew like lemonade parades.
Chasing bugs with speedy feet,
In nature's play, oh what a treat!

## Blossoms of the Mind's Eye

In gardens where dreams like daisies sprout,
I wear my thinking cap and dance about.
The bees all buzz in suits of bright plaid,
And every thought I have is not too bad.

A sunflower winks with a silly grin,
While dandelions play where the fun begins.
My mind throws petals, one by one,
Till giggles erupt, as bright as the sun.

## The Secret Language of Flowers

Roses whisper secrets in the breeze,
Tulips laugh at ants with such great tease.
Violets chat in shades of purple hue,
While lilacs roll their eyes, like flowers do.

A daisy giggles, 'Oh what a sight!'
While orchids argue who's the most polite.
Sunflowers nod, they're in on the joke,
The lilies burst out laughing, nearly choke.

**Petals in the Wind**

Petals fly by, like they're on a spree,
With pollen jokes as light as can be.
They tickle your nose, they swirl and spin,
As little bees buzz, inviting the din.

In gusty giggles, the petals dance,
Each twirl and swoop, a floral romance.
They twine through the air, no hint of a care,
While skies above chuckle, it's all quite rare.

## An Ode to Color and Light

In hues so vivid, like a painter's dream,
Colors get together, or so it would seem.
Yellow plays tag with a bright shade of blue,
While orange tries to outshine the crew.

In laughter they bloom, a riotous sight,
As every shade battles with joy and delight.
With splashes and swirls, they twirl all around,
Creating a ruckus, a jubilant sound.

## Colorful Reverie

In a garden full of cheer,
A purple daisy dressed in beer.
The butterflies do bicycle races,
While ants wear tiny shoelace faces.

The tulips threw a party loud,
They invited every flower crowd.
With balloons made of dandelion fluff,
They danced all night till their roots got tough.

A sunbeam slipped on the grass,
And what a funny sight it was!
It tickled the noses of all nearby,
As the daisies giggled and tried to fly.

A ladybug took charge of fate,
Said, 'Let's all make a silly gait!'
They pranced and hopped, oh what a show,
Even the fence posts joined in the row.

## The Artistry of Nature

In this gallery of green delight,
Painted petals shine so bright.
The roses blushed as bees took flight,
'We're the stars of the night!' they bite.

An artist squirrel with a paint can,
Drew a portrait of a leaf: simple plan.
But the wind swirled it all away,
Now it's just a game they play.

A daffodil wore a funny hat,
Claimed it was for the chitchat.
While clovers hovered like little fans,
Cheering on their garden plans.

In every nook, a laugh erupts,
As nature weaves and spins their cups.
Through all the giggles of the trees,
A laughter blooms like buzzing bees.

## **Touch of Sunlight on Petals**

A droplet of dew, a morning tease,
Sipping sunshine from floweresque breeze.
The daisies chat, oh what a yarn,
They claim to dance with the sun on the lawn.

The marigolds giggle, their heads held high,
Tickling the clouds as they wave bye-bye.
With a flick of their petals, they catch a breeze,
Engaging the butterflies in comical sleaze.

Lazily lounging, the violets doze,
Roused by the laughter where the sunflower grows.
Mirths of sunlight play hide and seek,
While petals wear socks - so unique!.

With a wink, a bloom says, 'Oh dear,
Why does the wind always tickle my ear?'
The garden's alive with bloomin' fun,
Chasing the giggles 'til day is done.

## Luminous Garden Tales

In shadows where the critters play,
A sour grape tried to make a gay.
With laughter loud, it slipped and fell,
The tomatoes snickered, 'Oh, do tell!'

A celery stick with a twinkle proud,
Led the veggies in a goofy crowd.
They waltzed about with colorful spoons,
Singing songs to the laughter of moons.

The mushrooms played hide and seek,
While carrots dressed as kings quite sleek.
With hats made of petals and capes of leaves,
They plotted their fun in the evening eves.

The sun dipped low, the stars took flight,
As night creeps in, they shine so bright.
Nature's comedy, in full display,
In the garden, everyone's here to play.

**Serenity in Blooming Whispers**

In a garden where giggles grow,
Flowers dance, putting on a show.
Bees wear sunglasses, buzzing with flair,
Counting the petals, they'd never dare!

The daisies gossip, oh what a sight,
"Did you hear, the sun's feeling bright!"
Tulips turn heads, a jealous affair,
While lazy lilacs just lounge in their chair.

## Cascade of Celestial Colors

In a sky painted with twilight dreams,
Pansies chuckle and plot their schemes.
A dandelion with a big toothy grin,
Dares the wind to join in its spin!

Sunflowers wager on topsy-turvy spins,
Who's the tallest? Oh, let the games begin!
Petals like confetti, joyfully thrown,
In this meadow, laughter has grown.

## Petal Rain: A Tapestry Unfolds

When petal rain begins to fall,
Every flower giggles, just giving their all.
Daffodils dance in their bright yellow shoes,
While violets chase 'round, sharing their news!

Butterflies waltz in the misty air,
Each twirl a challenge, light as a feather.
The whole field laughs, a riotous scene,
A tapestry of joy, serene yet keen!

## **The Illuminated Rose**

A rose with a glow, what a funny sight,
Winking at bees and feeling quite bright.
"Oh look at me!" it proudly proclaims,
"Dare you to guess my fancy names?"

With thorns like jokes, sharp yet so sweet,
It pricks at laughter, never admits defeat.
Gardening gloves sharing tales at twilight,
In the midst of petals, all feels just right.

## A Mosaic of Floral Delight

In the garden, colors play,
Petals giggle, dance away.
Bees wear hats, so round and bright,
They buzz to tunes of pure delight.

Daisies hide in bright green grass,
While rude sunflowers start to sass.
Tulips gossip, bloom with pride,
While lazy roses just abide.

Lilies laugh at jokes we tell,
Violets bloom, they wish us well.
The pansies wink from every side,
In this place where joy can't hide.

So come, my friends, let's have some fun,
In a world where flowers run.
With laughter ringing from above,
Nature's humor is true love.

## **Palette of the Sunlit Meadows**

A brush of colors on the plain,
With splashes bright, we go insane.
The poppies cheer, they strut with flair,
While clovers play hide and seek with air.

Buttercups laugh, they've got the moves,
While dandelions sport their grooves.
The sun, a painter, bright and bold,
Makes every petal worth more than gold.

And oh, the daisies crack a joke,
Even the shyest stem will poke.
In meadows where the laughter rolls,
Every bloom has funny souls.

So grab a friend, come take a peek,
In this garden, funny and chic.
With petals dressed in colors wild,
Nature's canvas is truly styled.

## **The Dance of Vivid Petals**

Watch them twirl, the petals bright,
Dancing away in pure delight.
They shimmy left, then dip so low,
A floral show that steals the show.

Cacti attempt a clumsy jig,
While lilies sway, feeling quite big.
Iris joins, with grace in her step,
In this garden, there's no misstep.

The daisies giggle, take their chance,
While tulips try to pull a prance.
Laughing leaves in breezes swirl,
They dance as if they're in a whirl.

So let's rejoice, those petals grand,
In nature's dance, where all is planned.
With every step, a chuckle's found,
In this wild, vivid playground.

## Perfume of a New Dawn

The morning light with scents so sweet,
Teases our noses, a charming treat.
The flowers yawn, stretch out their arms,
While nectar sways with flowery charms.

A daffodil slips, falls on the dew,
Silly moments, so fresh and new.
The roses giggle, brush aside dust,
Sharing stories, in laughter, we trust.

Lavender whispers, "Let's be bold,"
As bees recount tales that they've told.
In the scent of blooms, we find the fun,
Mornings of mischief have just begun.

So breathe in deep, let the humor play,
In perfume dreams that greet the day.
With laughter lingering soft and warm,
Embrace the joys that nature will charm.

## Colors of the Unseen Night

In shadows where the laughter plays,
A polka-dotted world of quirky ways.
The moon, a comedian up on high,
Makes stars chuckle as they wink and sigh.

With every twinkle, jokes unfold,
Cosmic gags in a language bold.
Sunset slips with a giggle loud,
As darkness wears a charming cloud.

The breeze cracks jokes on the sly,
While fireflies share tales, oh my!
A canvas of mishaps, painted bright,
Where even the shadows take flight.

So raise a glass to the unseen cheer,
In this wild night, all joy draws near!
Beneath the giggling twinkling light,
We dance and laugh, oh what a sight!

## Soft Lumens in a Wild Terrain

In a jungle where the giggles grow,
Light beams dance and put on a show.
The vines wear hats, so out of place,
And trees don glasses with a grin on their face.

Mushrooms in polka dots, a true delight,
Frolic and twirl in the soft moonlight.
A raccoon with a top hat, struts with flair,
While fireflies are dancing without a care.

A babbling brook sings a silly tune,
While crickets harmonize with the moon.
This wild terrain beams with fun,
As laughter echoes, we unite as one.

In nature's pranks, the heart's embrace,
We find our place, and there's no race.
Chasing flashes, gentle and bright,
In this terrain, everything feels right!

## Awakening the Nightingale

When the stars finally start to chat,
A nightingale dons a superhero hat.
She tunes her voice, a comic delight,
And croons beneath the silver light.

The bushes laugh with a rustling cheer,
As she cracks jokes that everyone hears.
With each sweet note, the critters sway,
Whispering secrets in a quirky way.

Owls roll their eyes as she nails the punch,
While hedgehogs snicker, a giggling bunch.
Singing of cakes and bright purple goo,
Awakening joy in the evening dew.

In a symphony of quirky sounds,
The nightingale spreads laughter around.
Her song a map, guiding the glee,
In this wild concert, we're all fancy-free!

## **The Heart's Garden Illuminated**

In a garden where the laughter blooms,
Flowers wear hats and dance like looms.
The daisies gossip, petals all aflutter,
As bees wear bowties, mixing sweet with butter.

Each laugh tumbles from the sunflower's gaze,
With carrots cracking jokes in a playful haze.
The tulips twirl, glittering with prime,
Creating rhymes in vibrant time.

Worms in tuxedos serve jokes with glee,
As ladybugs giggle atop the trees.
A garden party, under the moon,
Where whimsy and joy are never done too soon.

So let's toast to the fun that we share,
In this silly place, without a care.
Where laughter grows, wild and free,
Our heart's garden shines, as bright as can be!

## A Symphony in the Garden

In a garden where carrots wear hats,
And the tomatoes just giggle like brats.
The cucumbers dance with such flair,
While the radishes plot a fresh scare.

A symphony plays from bees on the rise,
As the daisies and dandelions criticize.
With wormy debates on a leaf-lined stage,
Nature's comedians steal the age!

## Paintbrush of the Earth

The earth smiles wide in a palette of hues,
As flowers strut in their colorful shoes.
The sun spills laughter across the green,
While the bees do a jig, oh so keen!

Rabbits in bowties paint with glee,
As rainbows mix with a cup of tea.
With splashes of fun in each little nook,
The soil might just write a funny book!

## Harmonies of Nature's Palette

In a garden where colors collide,
A purple flower sprouted a smile wide.
The daisies giggled, the roses just blushed,
While sunflowers mocked the weeds in a hush.

Bees danced like they owed the place rent,
With pollen suits, they were over content.
A butterfly slipped, tripped on a rose,
And pollen sneezed, as if it could pose.

The daisies all showed off their new shades,
While tulips told jokes from the latest parades.
Even the thorns were grinning with glee,
In this patch of humor, wild and free.

## Flourishing Serenity

A cactus dreamed of a sandy retreat,
While ferns hosted parties with grass for a seat.
The lilacs debated on whom to ignore,
While the ocean breeze snickered and swore.

Napping was standard for lazy old shrubs,
As ladybugs gathered for laughter and rubs.
The sun peeked through clouds with a sultry grin,
Its rays played hopscotch, let the games begin!

The daisies wore sunglasses, stylish and bright,
While the morning dew sparkled, a wonderful sight.
With every new giggle, a new petal popped,
In this world of wonder, the humor never stopped.

## **Elegance in Full Blossom**

Orchids donned hats, strutting around,
While tulips played charades on the ground.
The violets whispered their latest gag,
As peonies tightened their floral swag.

In summer's warm embrace, laughter took flight,
With petals dancing under the moonlight.
A sunflower tried to paint a still life,
But ended up blank, which caused quite a strife.

Carnations complained about being ignored,
While poppies insisted they were adored.
Yet in this chaos, joy intertwined,
In nature's soirée, with love well-defined.

## Enchanted Floral Dance

In a wobbly twirl, the lilies pranced,
While daisies and pansies slowly chanced.
With polka-dotted petals, they shook with cheer,
As dandelion wishes floated near.

Frogs crooned opera by the pond's gentle curve,
While petals jumped in, with rhythmic verve.
The lavender rolled in laughter and flair,
As bees served drinks with a buzz in the air.

Every flower's gossip shared with delight,
As buds blushed crimson, a funny sight.
In this merry gathering, no dullness could stay,
For in this floral dance, humor leads the way.

## A Garden's Gentle Heart

In the garden, snails race fast,
While daisies giggle, holding their grasp.
Butterflies wear their best attire,
And worms break out into a choir.

A squirrel steals the gardener's hat,
While roses flirt with the lazy cat.
A sunflower winks with its bright face,
As bees buzz around in a buzzing race.

The carrots wear tiny shoes so cute,
While radishes strut in their earthy root.
Dandelions dance in the soft breeze,
Tickling the grass, oh what a tease!

Every flower holds a joke to share,
With laughter echoing everywhere.
In this garden, joy takes its place,
Creating smiles on each blooming face.

## Starlight in a Flower's Glow


At night, the buds put on a show,
Twinkling bright, they steal the glow.
Daisies in pajamas, ready to dream,
While peonies plot a moonlit scheme.

The tulips wear crowns made of light,
As nightingales croon till the dawn's sight.
Fireflies laugh in a flickering race,
Lighting up paths with their tiny grace.

Chubby frogs leap in leafy verse,
Reciting love lines, but things get worse!
For lilies giggle at their loud croak,
Water plants join in, with a mocking poke.

In this twilight, joy finds its way,
With every petal in bright display.
For even the stars envy the grace,
Of this garden's nighttime vibrant space.

## Nature's Resplendent Symphony

The trees conduct a silly tune,
Swaying left and right under the moon.
Leaves join in with a rustling cheer,
As crickets join the band, oh dear!

The birds take solos, all out of tune,
Fluttering about like a wild typhoon.
A squirrel plays the wooden flute,
As rabbits dance in fancy boots.

Sunflowers sway, their heads held high,
While daisies giggle, their petals sly.
The brook plays percussion, splish and splash,
As frogs leap high, making quite a crash.

In this concert, all's a delight,
With each plant swinging into the night.
For nature knows how to bring a laugh,
Creating a symphony with nature's craft.

## A Song of Colorful Horizons

Painted petals in wild array,
Laughing colors brightening the day.
Pansies tease with their cheeky grins,
While violet jokes spark playful wins.

At the edge of the garden, bold and spry,
Silly sunflowers reach for the sky.
Their heavy heads bobble left and right,
As perched butterflies join the light flight.

With crayon colors splashed with glee,
Even the weeds join in the spree.
Each stem and sprout, a comical sight,
Painting the canvas, how wonderfully bright!

In every corner, laughter flows,
As petals play tag with the garden's prose.
This vibrant orchestra, wide and free,
Turns every glance into joyful spree.

## **The Blooming Canvas**

In gardens bright, where colors clash,
A daisy wears a floppy sash.
The tulips giggle, sway, and prance,
While roses plot a sneaky dance.

With every hue, a tale to weave,
A sunflower's grin, who can believe?
The violets whisper, share a wink,
As bees get tangled in a drink.

Each petal shaped with whimsy's flair,
A portrait made with utmost care.
Yet squirrels laugh at what they see,
Their acorns plucked, all in a spree.

Oh what a sight, this vibrant show,
Where nature's brush paints high and low.
In playful hues, the world's a stage,
A garden filled with giggles, age to age.

**Nature's Coloring Book**

A page of green, a splash of red,
Where butterflies go paint their spread.
With crayons made from pollen gold,
The daisies write stories bold.

The maples scribble crazy lines,
While poppies bounce like jumping vines.
Each flower's wink a joke well played,
Upon this canvas, laughter laid.

The lilac laughs, a pastel shade,
Says, "Hey, let's join the grand parade!"
And daisies twirl in sunny glee,
As artists hum, 'Come laugh with me!'

With every stroke, a giggle blooms,
Within the laughter, no more glooms.
A world of color, pure delight,
That tickles hearts from morn till night.

## Reflecting in Petal Pools

In puddles bright, the petals float,
Reflecting jokes, a funny quote.
The lilies smirk, their leaves a crown,
While frogs wear ties and never frown.

A lively scene of water fights,
As dragonflies zoom in delights.
With ripples dancing, all around,
The jokes of flowers, they abound.

The buzzing bees share laugh-filled tales,
While lazy ants march on with wails.
"What's this? A pool!" the petals scream,
And cannonball in, a floral dream.

So join the fun where water plays,
And petals mirror sunny days.
For in this pool, joy does reside,
With laughter swimming side by side.

## Light's Caress on Floral Faces

When sunlight comes to give a tickle,
The flowers giggle, play a trickle.
A petal blushes, cheeky and bright,
As shadows dance in laughter's flight.

The roses play hide and seek,
While daisies shout, 'We're not so meek!'
The sunlight shines with silly grace,
As flowers laugh in bright embrace.

Each bloom a smile, a quirky face,
In gardens filled with bold, sweet space.
The morning dew, a jest so spry,
Catches whispers in the sky.

So let the light come play and tease,
Where every flower laughs with ease.
In nature's arms, fun intertwines,
As colors brighten with bright designs.

## The Essence of Spring

In the garden, a bee does dance,
Trying hard to find romance.
A tulip snickers, saying, "Please!"
While dodging pollen with such ease.

The daffodils wear silly hats,
While squirrels charm with their acrobats.
Each flower grinning, nature's joke,
As sunlight warms the playful oak.

The breeze whirls in a joyful spin,
Tossing petals, making them grin.
Grab a prune, the bird calls out,
For a spring party, there's no doubt!

Even raindrops join the spree,
Twirling down happily, you see.
So let's all laugh, take springtime's cue,
For there's fun in every bloom anew!

## Joy Unfurled in Petals

A petal flutters, hues so bright,
Dancing in the morning light.
"Look at me!" the jasmine beams,
"I'll take over your sweetest dreams!"

The roses chuckle, soft and sweet,
While tulips play hide-and-seek in heat.
"Catch me first!" they giggle low,
While daisies join the playful show!

Sunshine tickles every leaf,
Nature laughs without a grief.
The grass is green, so plush and thick,
As joyful critters play their trick!

Petals paint the world in fun,
Spring-time laughter has begun.
So lift your spirits, dance along,
In this floral festival, we belong!

## Fragrant Memories of Youth

A whiff of lilac brings a grin,
Recalling all the tricks and spins.
Kids in gardens, muddy shoes,
Searching for the best petal hues.

Dandelions, crowns on heads,
While parents sigh in flower beds.
"You've turned me into a lion!"
Squeals filled with absolute sublime!

Jumping puddles, oh what a mess,
Nature's laughter is the best.
We'd race the wind, the sun would cheer,
Squeezing memories year by year.

So here's to laughter in the breeze,
A fragrance of fun, if you please.
And as we age, let's not forget,
Those sweet scents of joy, never fret!

## **Between the Petals and the Sky**

Butterflies start their giggly flight,
Winking at flowers, quite a sight.
"Are you a star, or just a bloom?"
They ask each other, dodging gloom.

Up above, clouds play tricks on bees,
While crickets dance beneath the trees.
The colors clash in a playful row,
As laughter sparkles, roots will grow.

Frogs in the pond try out their croaks,
Swapping jokes with ancient oaks.
Each ripple echoes joy, you see,
While petals sway so carefree!

So look up high, or look down low,
Laughter's everywhere, in the flow.
Between the colors and the air,
Fun and joy are always there!

## Radiant Rebirth in Spring

The flowers woke from winter's nap,
The bees buzzed loud, a happy clap.
With crooked stems, the tulips sway,
And confusion reigns, in bright array.

The daisies giggle, the roses tease,
As pollen floats, a sneeze with ease.
The little buds in rowdy cheer,
Shout, "We were sleeping, now we're here!"

The sun, it tickles every petal,
While insects join in spring's great kettle.
A dance-off starts, the cacti cheer,
"Leave us alone, we're prickly here!"

With mud pies squished in joyful glee,
The nature pranksters count to three.
Spring amateurs bring out their best,
Forget to wear shoes to this fest!

## Luminous Threads of Nature

In the garden, the shadows play,
The sun's bright rays follow the sway.
Worms in top hats take a stroll,
While ladybugs form a rock 'n' roll.

The petals gossip, colors clash,
As butterflies perform a splash.
Moles in suits dig fancy holes,
While crickets sing their concert roles.

A spider spins a tangled web,
But oops! A breeze, it's lost its ebb.
The flowers laugh, their colors pop,
As bees in tuxedos do the bop.

The winds join in with silly tunes,
While frogs wear crowns and shake their goons.
Nature winks with twinkling sights,
A vibrant show of silly lights!

## Beneath Canopy of Light

Underneath the leafy dome,
The squirrels hold a baseball comb.
With acorns served on daisy plates,
They giggle at their friends' mistakes.

A sunbeam tickles every leaf,
As one young branch plays a big chief.
With shadows casting silly shows,
The forest floor becomes a prose.

The birds, they wear their finest hats,
Singing songs about the chats,
While rabbits hop in oversized shoes,
In this strange world, who's got the blues?

A patch of mushrooms starts a line,
With ants in line for something fine.
Nature's got a party vibe,
And laughter's rich, it won't prescribe!

## The Dance of Vibrant Fragrance

The scents collide, a fragrant fight,
With roses claiming they're most bright.
Lilies boast of elegance rare,
While sunflowers flaunt their golden hair.

The peonies twirl, a pirouette,
While daisies laugh, "You're not all set!"
A breeze appears to stir the pot,
"Each bloom's a king, give us a shot!"

In this wacky floral ball,
A wisteria flies, but will it fall?
With violets giggling, pulling pranks,
And orchids making silly flanks.

The perfume's thick with joyous cheer,
As bees hum tunes, a crowd so sincere.
"The dance must end?" one flower squeaks,
"Wait 'til next spring, we'll have new peaks!"

## Threads of Light in the Hush of Twilight

In twilight's gentle, dim embrace,
We dance around without a trace.
The fireflies strut their twinkly glow,
While crickets play a nightly show.

A cat's whisker tickles the air,
As shadows stretch without a care.
Laughter bubbles, firelight gleams,
Chasing down our silliest dreams.

A squirrel sneaks in, planning a raid,
On potato chips, the masquerade!
But he's caught by the dog's loud bark,
Who plays the role of the watchdog spark.

Under the stars, we break out snacks,
While plotting silly little pranks.
As moonbeams wink, we laugh and tease,
In twilight's arms, we find our ease.

## A Celestial Bloom Reverie

In gardens where the oddballs grow,
The tulips dance, putting on a show.
Petunias wear their brightest hue,
While daisies giggle, 'How do you do?'

A gnome with style, a hat so fine,
He strikes a pose—it's all divine!
With scent of cookies in the breeze,
We munch them down, just with such ease.

The stars peek down, they want to cheer,
While crickets whisper, 'Not too near!'
Yet we trip on roots and laugh so loud,
In this green wonder, we feel so proud.

With quirky hats and outfits grand,
We frolic 'round in nature's land.
The night goes on, our laughter rings,
Under celestial blooms, oh how it sings!

## **Petals of Radiance**

In fields where colors start to play,
The flowers wink, and sway away.
A daffodil shimmies, it's got no shame,
While daisies giggle, 'Don't you dare blame!'

A bumblebee buzzes, quite the flirt,
Around the blossoms, where it can't hurt.
Petals steal snacks, soft petals hoot,
As butterflies tease, donning nice boots.

We gather petals, quite a rare sight,
To trade for magic under moonlight.
The petals scatter like confetti so bright,
In our hopscotch game, oh what a delight!

As tulips tell tales of gossip and cheer,
And violets plot mischief, you can hear.
Under the sun and the shining moon,
Our garden's a sitcom, seasons in tune!

## **Luminescent Flora**

In gardens where the odd critters play,
Glow-in-the-dark flowers sway all day.
Lollipops bloom and chocolate leaves sprout,
Nature's candy land, there's no doubt!

A ladybug dons a little fedora,
While beetles tango, 'Let's do the hora!'
With petals giggling in dazzling hues,
We join the dance, and wiggle our shoes.

The moon peeks in, with a brightened grin,
Bats throw confetti—let the fun begin!
We play hide and seek, amongst the trees,
While owls hoot softly, 'Oh come, if you please!'

The night unfolds, it's time to feast,\nWith fruit bat friends, we join the beast.
So here's to the flora, glowing and grand,
In this silly world, we all take a stand!

## **Glistening Petals and Skyward Dreams**

In the garden, bees wear hats,
Dancing to the tune of chubby chats.
Flowers giggle, swaying on a breeze,
Tickling the air, oh what a tease!

Squirrels don tuxedos, so spry and bright,
Stealing seeds, oh what a sight!
They wrestle with thorns, but can't get far,
Each tumble a tumble, each leaf a star.

Bright daisies wink in the golden sun,
Who knew that blooming could be such fun?
"Tickle me pink!" one lilac screamed,
While roses swayed, they all just dreamed.

The sunflowers sported shades so cool,
Playing hopscotch, breaking every rule.
With laughter ringing through the sunny morn,
Who knew plants could be so brightly born?

## The Color of Awakening

Waking blooms with sleepy yawns,
Butterflies prance on dew-kissed lawns.
Tulips in pajamas laugh and play,
In their frocked colors, bright as day.

The daffodils crack jokes on the vine,
Telling tales of fish that can't entwine.
They chuckle and giggle, sharing inside cheer,
While snails race slow, saying, "Not this year!"

With every petal fluffed and poised,
A garden that's simply overjoyed.
Nature's chatter sets the tone,
In this riot of hues, we are never alone.

As colors throng, all bright and merry,
The wind joins in with a good old ferry.
In this riotous realm of flora and glee,
Every shade's a guest at our fun jubilee!

## **Enchanted Petal Pathways**

Along the path where petals grin,
A parade of pollen spin begins.
Grass blades wiggle with a twist and shout,
Celebrating spring with a happy clout.

Ladybugs in hats push marigold carts,
Selling laughter and polka-dot arts.
The branches sway in a lively sync,
While flowers sip nectar and do a twink!

Dandelions wear crowns, feeling so grand,
Crowning the mushrooms, a mishap at hand.
"Mushrooms can dance better than you!" they jest,
But toadstools just nod, thinking they're blessed.

With each step forward, stories unfold,
Of petals that dance and blossoms that bold.
In this joyful journey of color and cheer,
Floral adventures bring us all near!

## Gentle Whispers of Floral Vitality

Whispers of petals fill the air,
Flower talk is quite the affair!
Sunlight trickles, tickling feet,
While pollen plays hide-and-seek on a beat.

The violets gossip, sharing the news,
"Did you see the roses in sparkly shoes?"
With a wink of the sun and a nudge of a breeze,
Gardeners giggle, planting their tease.

"Let's paint the fence with colors bright,
Every shade should dance in the light!"
Tulips twirl with such flair and grace,
Turning the garden into a race.

As laughter grows among petals bright,
Every bloom joins in the laughter's delight.
In this enchanted bloom of vibrant spree,
Each whisper felt is a blossom's decree!

## **Petals Unfurled Under the Sun**

Under the sun, they dance and sway,
A silly waltz in bright array.
With bees that buzz, and ants that jive,
Who knew these flowers could come alive?

Dandelions flaunt their fluffy hair,
While tulips gossip without a care.
Hilarity blooms in the garden plot,
As petals giggle in cheerful knots.

The violets strike a pose so grand,
While daisies play a game so planned.
They chuckle as the wind blows strong,
In this botanical sitcom, they belong.

So if you wander where colors play,
Join the petals in their funny display.
For in the garden under the sun,
Each laugh and smile is pure, wild fun!

## The Harmony of Vibrant Life

In the garden of chaos, bees take flight,
Chasing each other till they lose sight.
Ladybugs laugh in their tiny suits,
While grasshoppers strut in their green boots.

The sunflowers pose, tall and bright,
Flexing their stems like a heavyweight fight.
With petals laughing and wagging their toes,
Are they blossoms or a circus? Who knows!

Butterflies flutter without a care,
Like fashion icons in the spring air.
They try on colors, mix and match,
Creating a scene the bees must catch.

So wander through this colorful spree,
Where flowers laugh so joyfully free.
In this vibrant life, don't forget to smile,
And stay for the show, it's worth your while!

## **A Palette of Spring's Delight**

Crayons of colors on nature's brush,
Looks like spring came with quite the crush.
Paint your troubles on petals so bright,
As laughter erupts from morning till night.

Lilies take selfies, tulips pose wide,
In this gallery, flowers take pride.
The wind whispers jokes, petals turn red,
As they chuckle together, no fear or dread.

Frogs in the pond croak a funny tune,
While butterflies dance, under the moon.
Nature's a painter, with laughter its hue,
Creating a scene that feels fresh and new.

So grab your palette, go paint the day,
Let the colors and giggles lead the way.
In the gallery of spring, let's all unite,
And share in the laughter till the stars ignite!

## Petals of Inspiration

In the garden of giggles, ideas bloom,
With petals whispering, dispelling gloom.
They chatter and chuckle with whimsical grace,
As creativity blossoms in every space.

Mossy comedians on rocks so round,
Cracking jokes that only plants have found.
With roots in the soil and their heads in the sky,
Everyone's laughing, oh my, oh my!

The sun casts shadows, plays peek-a-boo,
Saying, "Hey there, flowers, let's create something new!"

With laughter as fuel, the ideas take flight,
Inspiration dances, oh what a sight!

So tiptoe through laughter and cherish each smile,
For inspiration's waiting, just stay for a while.
In this flowering comedy, let your heart soar,
With petals of wisdom opening doors!

# Fractals of Floral Dreams

In a garden where daisies dance,
We found a lost shoe, what a chance!
It sat there sulking, in the sun's beam,
A fashion statement, or so it seemed.

The sunflowers giggled, tall and bright,
While ants held parties, just out of sight.
Lettuce gossiping, lettuce affair,
Who knew veggies had such flair, I swear!

A talking rose recited a rhyme,
Claiming sprouting was a form of crime.
With honeybees buzzing in a huddle,
They plotted against a field's muddy puddle.

Each bloom had a tale, each petal a scheme,
In this whimsical patch, nothing's as it seems.
With laughter contagious, we took to the sky,
A parade of flowers, on dreams we fly!

## **Shimmering Echoes of the Heart**

In the meadow, a squirrel took a leap,
Landed on flowers that seemed half asleep.
The petals woke up, all fluffed and sassy,
Chasing him back with faces quite classy.

A butterfly twirled in a dress made of light,
But tripped on a daisy, oh what a sight!
With a flip and a flop, down it did plummet,
Landing smack dab on a surprised little summit.

The tulips erupted in laughter so loud,
Forming a chorus, a giggling crowd.
"Let's start a fashion show," a crocus did say,
While a dahlia posed in a most fab display!

Under the sun, the fun never wanes,
As petals find joy in absurd little gains.
A garden of chuckles, a playground divine,
Where even the weeds know how to shine!

## **Splendor in Soft Shadows**

In twilight's embrace, shadows grow tall,
Where daisies attempt to outshine it all.
An old oak tree sneezed, 'Achoo!' with a grin,
And squirrels flew, leaving giggles in the wind.

The lilies were whispering love notes in code,
While tulips were tossing an exciting abode.
"Let's play charades!" chimed in a brave fern,
As fireflies flickered, awaiting their turn.

A willow was weaving a story in sway,
With branches like arms that beckoned to play.
But one little petal tripped over a stone,
And landed quite splat on a joker's throne.

The moon peeked out, a smirk on its face,
As nightly antics took root in this place.
With giggles and chirps, the shadows recede,
In a botanical world, a laugh is the seed!

## The Symphony of Opening Buds

A bud stretched its limbs, in morning's embrace,
While a daffodil danced, in a rather odd pace.
"Keep it subtle!" a tulip did shout,
"Don't scare the bees; we need them about!"

A conga line started, from roots to the sky,
With daisies and dandelions hopping nearby.
"Join in the fun!" cried a bold little sprout,
As petals erupted, with laughter and shout.

The violets giggled, a prank on the air,
Covering sneezes with pastel-colored flair.
"Blow a kiss, make a wish!" a cheerful rose laughed,
While a bumblebee buzzed, quite happily daft.

Each bloom a diva, with antics galore,
In this garden stage, never a bore.
With petals uniting, they sang loud and free,
In a symphony sweet, of color and glee!

## Garden of Shimmering Dreams

In a garden, the gnomes dance around,
Sipping nectar with faces quite round.
They giggle at daisies, all dressed in white,
Under the sun, they twirl with delight.

The tulips gossip, oh what a scene,
Trading secrets on what they have seen.
A rose told a joke, petals shook with glee,
Laughter echoed beneath the green tree.

Bumblebees buzz with their swaggering style,
Chasing butterflies, running a mile.
They bump into blooms, oh dear, what a mess,
As pollen flies high, they just laugh and confess.

At dusk, they toast with their finest brew,
To the quirks of flowers that bloom in the dew.
Every leaf sways, a wild feathered dance,
In this garden of dreams, seize every chance.

## Fragrant Whispers in Bloom

In the meadow where confetti flowers spin,
A sunflower whispers, 'Let the fun begin!'
Turnips wear sunglasses, all laid-back and chill,
While carrots debate if they're better than dill.

A peony giggles at a bluebird's song,
Claiming it knows the words all along.
Pansies jest about the weather and rain,
With petals that flutter, they dance the refrain.

As dusk falls near, a clover starts pranks,
Hiding under leaves, giving raucous thanks.
The daisies all snicker, 'Oh, what a sight!'
As the stars peek through, their laughter takes flight.

In this fragrant world with whimsy aflow,
Every bloom knows just how to steal the show.
With petals and giggles, the night takes a bow,
Nature's great theater, there's humor, somehow.

## **Vibrant Awakening**

In the early dawn, the flowers yawn wide,
A sleepy petunia slid down for a ride.
The hyacinths giggle, exposed to the sun,
As marigolds joke, 'We're brighter, you pun!'

A squirrel scurries with a nut in its mouth,
Poking for mischief, heading due south.
He trips on a daisy, her laughter erupts,
While tulips all chuckle, in giggles they're cupped.

The violets whisper, 'What's that in a crook?'
A butterfly bobbed, with a casual look.
Spreading their wings, all colorful blends,
They swirl through the garden, the best of friends.

With every new bloom, the laughter does swell,
A symphony symphony of nature that tells.
'The world's full of fun, let's bloom and explore!'
In this vibrant land, there's always much more!

## The Radiant Orchard

In the orchard of giggles, the apples all grin,
Crisp leaves are blushing, and so is the skin.
A peach takes the leap, 'Catch me if you dare!'
While cherries just bounce in the open air.

The branches tell stories of fruit in the breeze,
Of honeybee antics, and wild honey tease.
With plums that are spinning in a spirited whirl,
Even grapes join the fun, giving life a twirl.

Blackberries cackle with a juicy delight,
Sipping sweet nectar far into the night.
They paint nightly tales with their juicy zest,
In this radiant grove, laughter's always the best!

So come take a stroll where the fruit laughs in cheer,
Join the joyful rhythm that is always near.
In this magical orchard, all worries take flight,
Every fruit's just a jest in the soft moonlight.

## Symphony of Colorful Petals

In a garden where giggles grow,
The flowers dance in a vibrant show.
Sunflowers waltz in the warm sunlight,
While daisies play hide-and-seek at night.

Bumblebees wear tiny top hats,
Sipping nectar, they're quite the chitchats.
Rosebuds gossip, their petals unfold,
In a language only flowers can hold.

Tulips hop and the violets cheer,
With jokes that tickle, drawing us near.
Laughter echoes as petals sway,
In this garden, who needs a bouquet?

Each bloom's a punchline, a colorful jest,
They tickle our souls and invite us to rest.
So join the fun, let your worries flee,
In this playful garden, you'll giggle with glee!

## **Illuminated Garden Paths**

Along the paths where the lanterns shine,
Frogs in tuxedos sip on sweet brine.
The moonlight winks at the flowers' dance,
While fireflies twirl in a merry prance.

Caterpillars wear glasses, quite astute,
Debating which leaf they should call cute.
A pumpkin carriage rolls with a funny hum,
And sings to the flowers, 'Here's where I'm from!'

The hedgehogs play cards, their spines in a row,
While crickets recite poems, a talented show.
Laughter rings out under starlit skies,
A party in petals, where silliness lies.

These paths invite, with their quirky flair,
Join in the laughter; no worries to spare.
In this garden of humor, bright as a star,
Each step reveals joy from those near and far!

## Dreams Woven in Petals

In slumbering petals, the dreams take flight,
With giggles of grasshoppers sounding just right.
Under moonbeams, daisies weave tales,
Of unicorns prancing, and windy gales.

Ladybugs dine on sweet aphid cakes,
Telling the roses about mistaken shakes.
With rhymes of giggles, dreams intertwine,
In this whimsical world, everything's fine.

Petals whisper secrets of raucous delight,
As the night blooms raucous with laughter so bright.
A mischievous breeze blows the dreams all around,
Carrying chuckles through the garden unbound.

From poppies to pansies, a comedy spree,
In each tiny flower, a wild laugh we see.
So gather your dreams, let them show you the way,
In a world of petals, where fun's here to stay!

## **Resplendent Flora**

In a garden where laughter spills on the ground,
Flora holds a court where giggles abound.
The daisies hold scepters, crowns made of leaves,
As they tease the tulips about their big sleeves.

The lilies recite the most silly of rhymes,
Timing their jokes to the chimes of the climes.
Cacti wear sombreros, swaying with flair,
While the poppies cheer on with contagious air.

Petunia pranksters sneak up with delight,
Sprinkling laughter like dew in the night.
Oh, how they cackle, those resplendent blooms,
Creating a world filled with whimsical tunes.

Join the festivities of this vibrant show,
As petals and giggles put on a grand glow.
In this splendid garden, come dance and explore,
For every small bloom holds a joke at its core!

## A Garden Awash in Color

In a garden where clowns grow tall,
The daisies giggle, bouncing their ball.
Roses wear glasses, all prim and neat,
While sunflowers dance on their eight tiny feet.

Bees wear top hats, buzzing in time,
They waltz with the flowers, a floral rhyme.
The tulips tell jokes, all in good cheer,
As butterflies laugh with a swish of their rear.

Lettuce is lounging, sipping on mint,
Radishes joke, 'We never grow stint!'
A riot of colors, nature's own spree,
In this leafy circus, wild and free.

So come to the garden, bring laughter and cheer,
Where petals are playful and joy's always near.
In this patch of delight, your troubles will cease,
With blooms that are bright and spirits that lease.

## The Veil of Colorful Dreams

In fields where the rainbows tumble and play,
The daffodils jest, brightening the day.
With tulips in tutus, they leap and they twirl,
While the daisies gossip, oh what a whirl!

Clouds wear suspenders, all fluffy and white,
As violets whisper, 'This is pure delight!'
The poppies, quite cheeky, stick out their tongues,
While peonies chuckle, their joy still unsung.

A squirrel in a party hat dashes on by,
With acorns for snacks, oh my, oh my!
They play hide and seek with the shadows of trees,
While the breeze carries laughter and tickles the leaves.

So dream in this realm, where humor's a trend,
The colors conspire, all sorrows suspend.
In this vibrant tapestry, let worries dissolve,
As laughter and whimsy together evolve.

## The Radiance of Nature's Heart

Where petals are painted in absurd delight,
The lilies tell stories that last through the night.
Bees wear capes, oh what a sight to behold,
While the thistles tease, 'We're not quite that bold!'

A crabapple tree throws a fruit cocktail bash,
As children sit under, all giggles and laughs.
The honeysuckle vine sings a catchy tune,
While tulips clink glasses beneath a bright moon.

The sun, in a hat, shines golden and bright,
While daisies hold hands, wishing on light.
In this garden of glee, where laughter abounds,
The petals are vibrant, joy's all around.

So skip through the meadow, let mirth be your mark,
Where nature's own jesters ignite a new spark.
With whimsy and wonder, let your spirits soar,
In this radiant realm, there's always more.

## The Flourishing Dreamscape

In a dreamscape where laughter takes flight,
The roses debate on who's funniest tonight.
They giggle and snicker, all in good jest,
While willow trees whisper, 'We are the best!'

Chrysanthemums chuckle, their colors so bright,
While hydrangeas giggle under stars of light.
Pansies wear hats, quite hip and trendy,
And dandelions blow puffs, all loose and bendy.

Ants in a cha-cha parade down a path,
With ladybugs cheering, joining the math.
The moon winks an eye, and the stars twirl around,
In this landscape of fun, sweet humor is found.

So dance with the flowers, let your spirits lift,
Embrace the enchantment, it's nature's gift.
In this world painted vivid with silly delight,
Live life like a party, let joy be your right.

## The Dance of Colorful Seasons

In spring, the flowers sway and grin,
The daisies wiggle, it's time to spin.
The tulips shout, 'We are the best!'
While sunflowers boast in a leafy fest.

Summer joins with rays so bright,
Bees buzzing loudly, oh what a sight!
Petunias laugh in their brightest hues,
As squirrels don shades and dance in their shoes.

Autumn winks with a leaf parade,
Pumpkins chuckle in a cozy shade.
The trees do a jig, all dressed in gold,
While critters hoard nuts, so bold and so bold.

Winter whispers, "I'm still around,"
With frosty jokes that dance on the ground.
Snowflakes twirl, such graceful tricks,
As hot chocolate sips from mugs make us grin.

## **Horizons Drenched in Bloom**

The sun spills laughter across the field,
A riot of colors, nature's shield.
Roses gossip, 'Look at us shine!'
While bees break dance, all feeling divine.

Tulips tease with their tall, proud heads,
As violets giggle in purple beds.
There's a daffodil boogie, who's got the moves?
While butterflies play, and the whole world improves.

Forget-me-nots whisper secrets so sweet,
Their tiny blossoms dance to the beat.
Ladybugs prance, oh, what a sight,
In this festival of color, pure delight!

Even the wind takes a playful spin,
As petals swirl, and laughter begins.
Horizons bloom in a riot divine,
Nature's comedy without a line.

## Nature's Kaleidoscope

A painter swings with a brush of glee,
Colors tumble down from the sky, you'd agree!
Lilies stretch out, trying to impress,
While garden gnomes giggle in their bright red dress.

Dandelions puff in a huff and a puff,
Spreading wishes that are silly and tough.
Blues and yellows make quite a scene,
While ants form a conga, moving in between.

The sun winks down, tickling the leaves,
While crickets chirp ballads of autumn eves.
Grasshoppers hop with a cheerful tune,
As clouds play hide and seek with the moon.

A butterfly trip, oh what a flight,
In patterns that swirl, oh, what a sight!
Nature's prankster, painting the day,
In a kaleidoscope spun in a playful way.

## Embrace of Floral Light

Daisies and poppies share the stage,
As blooming laughter spills from the page.
Violets wink, throwing a party,
While bumblebees dance, forever so hearty.

The breeze is tickling all around,
As sunbeams giggle, never profound.
Lilacs swirl in a fragrant whirl,
Spreading joy with every twirl.

A whimsical garden full of cheer,
With flickering fireflies buzzing near.
Comically bright, the petals sway,
In the embrace of light, they play.

Nature's jesters in full display,
With laughter soaked in every ray.
In this floral world, we take delight,
A fun-loving bloom in the soft twilight.

## **A Garden's Whispering Heart**

In a garden where daisies giggle,
And tulips dance with every wiggle,
A butterfly flits with a cheeky grin,
Sipping nectar, oh where do I begin?

The daisies chatter, a gossiping crew,
While roses say, "Look at me, too!"
With every petal, a silly tale,
Of mischief and laughter that never goes stale.

Sunflowers stand tall, in silly poses,
Complaining about weeds and their funny dozes,
While daisies pop in to steal the show,
Pointing to bees with a clever "hello!"

In this garden of laughter, take a seat,
Where giggles and colors are a wondrous treat,
Every bloom has a tale, a chuckle to share,
Join in the fun, if you dare!

## Melodies of Nature's Colors

A purple hue sings out a tune,
While lemons drop in, dancing at noon,
With every shade, a giggle explodes,
Nature's palette brings joy in loads!

Cacti wear hats made of feathers,
Grasshoppers chat about their own matters,
The daisies debate the best kind of sun,
While tulips rave about their upcoming run!

A rainbow of laughter spills from the sky,
As snails hold a parade, oh my oh my,
Chirping crickets provide the beat,
In this colorful world, life's nothing but sweet!

Every color laughs and twirls about,
With petals that shimmer and sprout,
So grab your friends, let's paint the town,
In melodies of nature, we'll never frown!

## In the Shade of Blooming Dreams

Under the shade where flowers conspire,
Dandelions giggle, never tire,
While violets plot their grand escape,
From the sneaky beetles in this landscape!

The sun sneaks in, a mischievous tease,
While bark beetles buzz like, "We've got keys!"
With dreams of growing, they plot and they scheme,
In the vibrant shade of a flower-filled dream.

Lily pads hold a pool party spree,
With dragonflies buzzing, "Come dance with me!"
As shadows dance on the petals' delight,
Beneath the moon, silly dreams take flight.

In this secret hideaway, fun never ends,
Where flowers are giggles and sunshine lends,
So come join the mischief, let's make a team,
In the charming shade of blooming dream!

## **Radiant Fragrance of Joy**

Smells like mischief, a whiff of delight,
With lavender laughter wafting at night,
The roses wink and share a quick joke,
While daisies giggle, giving a poke!

Each scent tells a story, quirky and wild,
As bees drop by, like a curious child,
"Oh, what's that over there?" they've been told,
A riot of color, more precious than gold!

The fragrance of fun fills the balmy air,
With daisies twirling and bees in a flare,
Every petal's laugh is a fragrant tease,
In this world of joy, life's a breeze!

So if you're near, take a deep sniff,
Join in the laughter, let your mood lift,
As the blossoms share a chuckle or two,
In this radiant fragrance, there's fun just for you!

## Chasing Light through Leafy Canopies

Squirrels in a race up high,
Chasing shadows as they fly.
Sunbeams dance on leafy beds,
While butterflies wear tiny spreads.

Laughter echoes, birds all cheer,
Nature's sitcom, bright and clear.
A chipmunk thinks it's time to nap,
While flowers giggle, giving a clap.

Why do the trees wear suits of green?
To show off their charm, so keen!
The sun peeks in with a graceful grin,
Who knew a forest could be this thin?

With every rustle, joy takes flight,
Under the canopy, all feels right.
So grab a snack, let's take a seat,
Nature's humor is quite the treat!

## Dawn's Brushstrokes on Petal Tides

Morning spills its orange hue,
While flowers wake from dreams anew.
Petals yawn and stretch quite wide,
As bumblebees begin to glide.

The tulips swirl in early light,
Dancing to a silent sight.
Oh, what fun to wake and sway,
As the sun insists, 'Let's play today!'

A rose tells jokes, all in bloom,
While daisies giggle, filling the room.
Even the grass is swaying low,
Chasing the rays in a row to row.

So let's toast to the dawn's delight,
With nature's paints, oh what a sight!
Each petal shares its secret game,
At dawn's brushstrokes, nothing's the same!

## Harmonics of the Flowers' Spectacle

In gardens where humor sings so loud,
Flowers form a lively crowd.
Petunias strut with vibrant flair,
While violets giggle without a care.

The roses hum a poppy tune,
Bees join in, swaying to the moon.
Laughter blooms in every hue,
Nature jamming, all for you!

Each blossom shares a wacky tale,
Of wind's wild dance and the nightingale.
Forget the stage; the flower's the star,
In this funny show, who needs a car?

So join the fun, no need to fret,
In petals' laughter, there's joy to get.
With nature's choir, let's sing it loud,
In a symphony where blooms are proud!

## The Alchemy of Waxing Petals

Under the sun, where laughter brews,
Petals shimmer in colorful hues.
Nature's alchemist stirs with glee,
Transforming buds into comedy.

Daffodils sport their golden hats,
While daisies prance and wiggle like cats.
Tulips toss jokes, oh what a sight,
Turning the garden into delight!

With each full bloom, a jest appears,
Giggling flowers dispel all fears.
What's that? A bee in a tuxedo?
Magic events are on the go!

So let's celebrate petals that shine,
In a world where laughter intertwines.
With nature's funny flair on display,
Join in the joy, come what may!

www.ingramcontent.com/pod-product-compliance
Ingram Content Group UK Ltd.
Pitfield, Milton Keynes, MK11 3LW, UK
UKHW021445290125
4349UKWH00039B/628